THIS JOURNAL NOTEBOOK BELONG

C000053434

_____

_____

FROM: _____

_____

BRICKSHUB

About Brickshub
Brickshub is a design company based in England. We specialize in custom apparel, personalized products, and branded merchandise. We understand that we're not just designing shirts, jewelry, footwear, watches, journals, tote bags, drinkware, or home accessories; we are helping people make memories. They're keepsakes that will remain with you for years to come.

Thank you for being our customer and for allowing us the opportunity to be of service.

Printed in Germany
by Amazon Distribution
GmbH, Leipzig